You Cor

MW01514346

The Art
of Influence

reaching the world through creativity and the Gospel

Matt Kramer

. . .Every gifted artisan in whom the Lord has put wisdom and understanding. . . .shall do according to all that the Lord has commanded.
Exodus 36:1

The Christian is the one whose imagination should fly beyond the stars.
Francis Schaeffer

A VERY BRIEF HISTORY

The beginning of a story is very important. Any writer will tell you that the opening paragraph of a book, the opening scene of a movie, the first few minutes of a play, or the first few notes of a song will determine whether you allow yourself to be drawn into the work of art or whether you will dismiss it.

God chose to begin *our* story- the story of humankind and the universe we were created in- with "In the beginning, God created the heavens and the earth."

This is perhaps the greatest opening line in the history of, well, not only the universe, but eternity itself.

In one simple sentence, we learn:

- that God is a master creator, and the sole creator of the universe we exist in

- that there is a beginning to the story of humankind, which means there will be a middle and ultimately, a conclusion

- that God is not only responsible for the creation of the stars and planets of our own physical universe, but of heaven and the eternal, supernatural realm

And like all great authors, He puts intrigue in the opening line, as well.

Why did He create this universe?

The fact that He was already in existence beforehand reveals His superiority over the laws of time and space. So what was He doing before the creation of our universe?

In fact. . . .who in the world is this God??

We have no choice. We're hooked and we *have* to read on. The story is not only told in the Bible, but in history itself. Despite critical opinions that state the Bible is full of errors, there is no other book in the world that can be verified *more* than the Bible, with tens of thousands of historical documents proving its accuracy, along with geological, scientific, and archeological evidence.

But then there's the believer in Christ, who believes in something more than just the historical validity of the Bible. The believer not only believes, but *knows* the Bible to be the Word of God, because Jesus is the Living Word (John 1), and because the believer knows Jesus, he or she knows that the Word is alive and active (Hebrews 4:12). It is an experiential reality.

We are all characters in this great story, a real story that continues to unfold every day of our lives.

But for the sake of this book, the central idea is that we know for a fact that God is a creative God. He says so in

His opening sentence. In a manner of speaking, it's how He introduces Himself in the story.

The introduction of characters is another important aspect of storytelling, and God and His Son Jesus have two of the most classic intros. God bursts into the story in a wildly exciting action sequence, while Jesus has the quietly understated entrance.

In short, God knows how to craft a story because He's done it since the beginning of time and is still doing it today. To quote Shakespeare, "All the world's a stage, and all the men and women merely players; they have their exits and their entrances."

Believing in the creative nature of God sounds basic, but if you don't believe that God is a creative God, then you won't understand why He wants to use it.

And why it's a shame that so few people *do* use it for His glory.

Art is one of the most influential mediums in Western civilization. And the term *art* is used in this book to encompass *all* forms of the Arts- cinema, theatre, books, music, painting, and so on- not just literal artwork.

Due to You Connection being mostly a media and theatre company, my discussion will also tend to focus more on the areas of performing and visual art, the kind involving actors and stages and cameras and presentations. It is this area of the Arts that I believe suffers the most from a lack of proper Christian influence, more so than painting, books, or music. (Christian music is quite a thriving industry that has truly embraced all styles of music in its evangelistic purposes, and the world of Christian fiction is, in my opinion, excellent, also embracing all forms of genres and literary styles.)

Christian films tend to suffer from a lack of creativity (and sometimes lack of quality in writing and acting), failing to appeal to certain viewers (Christian or otherwise) who prefer diverse or imaginative stories, genres, or styles.

As for live theatre, is the term *Christian theatre* even a thing?

Due to its frequent association throughout history with the secular side of life- Greeks, Romans, gypsies, saloons, music halls, pop music, Hollywood, Broadway- the Arts is rarely associated with the Bible-believing Christian faith. Historically, the Christian church has shunned the Arts as works of the devil, from the Puritans to some Christians in the 1970s who claimed rock music and electric guitars were only "the devil's music".

John Bunyan, who authored *The Pilgrim's Progress* in 1678, was one of the earliest Christians to pioneer the use of creativity to depict and discuss biblical theology, as well as making great advancements in society itself; *Pilgrim's Progress* is cited as the first English-speaking novel ever!

George MacDonald (1824-1905) was a Scottish author and minister who further pioneered using storytelling as a way of presenting biblical ideas, in such novels as *Phantastes, At the Back of the North Wind*, and *The Princess and the Goblin.* He is also cited as an early pioneer of fantasy literature, greatly influencing later Christian writers like C.S. Lewis, J.R.R. Tolkien, and Oswald Chambers (as well as many secular authors like Lewis Carroll, L. Frank Baum, Lloyd Alexander, Neil Gaiman, etc.).

MacDonald came from a family of book readers and was appalled that so many people of his day did not read books or know anything about Scottish or British folklore. It is amazing that in addition to using his stories for a spiritual purpose, he was also using them in a practical way, to help reintroduce reading and folktales to the culture around him. He is credited as the one who encouraged Lewis Carroll (a.k.a. Charles Dodgson) to professionally publish *Alice's Adventures in Wonderland.*

C.S. Lewis (1898-1963) was perhaps one of the greatest Christian writers and theologians of the 20th Century, and his works like *The Chronicles of Narnia, Out of the Silent Planet*, and *The Screwtape Letters* still reveal the power of using art as a means of presenting, explaining, and advancing the Gospel of Jesus Christ.

The Jesus Movement of the 1960s and 1970s introduced Christian rock and contemporary Christian music. The idea of using pop music to evangelize or preach the Gospel was very "out there" and radical in its day.

Frank Peretti reinvented the Christian fiction genre in literature with *This Present Darkness* and *Piercing the Darkness*, which presented the supernatural world with such shocking reality that these remain some of the greatest works of Christian fiction of all time.

Recent decades have seen the rise of Christian filmmaking, fueled by the phenomenal success of Mel Gibson's *The Passion of the Christ* in 2004 and Alex Kendrick's 2006 *Facing the Giants*, the latter of which demonstrated how a low-budget, independent Christian film could be financially successful. Both these films also revealed that there is a sizable audience for Christian Arts. These films paved the way for the eventual boom in online streaming sites like Pure Flix. *VeggieTales* (beginning in the 1990s) also proved that Christian Arts could be commercially successful and on par with Kermit the Frog and Mickey Mouse.

But as great as these influential figures and projects are, they are sadly few and far between when compared to other advancements the Christian church has made, in missionary work, politics, or the family sphere.

The truth is, all the other mountains of influence command much more of the church's time, energy, and resources. The Arts remains a strange, surreal world that only certain right-brained people understand. The vast majority of Christians think of the Arts as *entertainment only*, and there are many churchgoers who still tend to think of art as "secular and pagan", particularly when it involves certain styles of music, certain aesthetics, or imaginative elements like whimsy and fantasy.

And although there has been a rise in Christian entertainment, much of it has a tendency to be shallow or simply inspirational, not challenging viewers, listeners, or readers in the same way that a sermon would, or the Bible itself!

Christian films in particular tend to be safe, squeaky clean, and in the style of an inspirational Hallmark Channel movie, with characters who look like they are going to Sunday morning church and average, everyday problems that are solved safely, happily, and inspirationally by the conclusion.

But there is a portion of the population (Christian and non-Christian) that greatly responds to the Arts, *and there is so much more potential that the Christian church has yet to realize!*

Art doesn't have to just be entertainment, and it doesn't have to simply be inspirational. Creativity is a powerful tool that goes far beyond conventional methods of communication, tapping into the right brain- imagination, emotion, feeling, intuition, perception. And figures like John Bunyan, George MacDonald, and C.S. Lewis proved that we can push beyond the barriers of dull, linear methods and "go wild"! God is a creative God, and we can tap into that same unbridled creativity, and use the medium to not only communicate the Gospel, but to radically advance the kingdom of God with the same effectiveness as the other mountains of influence.

KEY SCRIPTURES:

Genesis 1 *(detailing the immense power of God's supernatural creativity)*

Romans 1:20 – *For since the creation of the world His invisible attributes are clearly seen, being understood by the things that are made, even His eternal power and Godhead, so that they are without excuse. . . .*

Psalms 19:1 – *The heavens declare the glory of God; and the firmament shows His handiwork.*

Colossians 1:16 – *For by Him all things were created that are in heaven and that are on earth, visible and invisible, whether thrones or dominions or principalities or powers. All things were created through Him and for Him.*

Philippians 2:13 – *For it is God who works in you both to will and to do for His good pleasure.*

2 Corinthians 10:4 – *For the weapons of our warfare are not carnal but mighty in God for the pulling down of strongholds, casting down arguments and every high thing that exalts itself against the knowledge of God, bringing every thought into captivity to the obedience of Christ.*

Exodus 36:1 – *Every gifted artisan in whom the Lord has put wisdom and understanding, to know how to do all man-*

ner *of work for the service of the sanctuary, shall do according to all the Lord has commanded.*

1 Corinthians 12:4-6 *– There are diversities of gifts, but the same Spirit. There are differences of ministries, but the same Lord. And there are diversities of activities, but it is the same God who works all in all.*

1 Corinthians 12:12:20 *– But now there are many members, yet one body. And the eye cannot say to the hand, "I have no need of you"; nor again the head to the feet, "I have no need of you." No, much rather, those members of the body which seem to be weaker are necessary.*

Ephesians 6:11-13 *– Put on the whole armor of God, that you may be able to stand against the wiles of the devil. For we do not wrestle against flesh and blood, but against principalities, against powers, against the rulers of the darkness of this age, against spiritual hosts of wickedness in the heavenly places. Therefore take up the whole armor of God, that you may be able to withstand in the evil day, and having done all, to stand.*

HOW CREATIVITY WORKS

The Arts is included in one of the Seven Mountains of Influence in Western society:

Government

Economics

Religion (Faith & Spirituality)

Education

Family

Media (News)

Arts, Entertainment, & Celebration

These are considered the key areas in Western civilization that have the most profound influence over humanity at large.

Government obviously determines the freedoms, norms, provisions, and indeed the quality of daily existence that a society will have.

Economics determines how much or how little a society will have to live by, which in turn determines the quality of living and the productivity of an entire nation.

Religion (or Faith & Spirituality, which is the terminology I prefer because it sounds less like a "stained glass window") is often listed at number three but ought to be number one (though a government can determine whether religion is allowed or outlawed, making it, at least in earthly terms, a more influential entity). "Every good and perfect gift is from above" (James 1:17), meaning God and His Word are the basis for everything. Therefore, whether a society honors or rejects God has a *huge* influence on how well that society will function, as history continues to prove.

Education determines the level of knowledge, intellect, and productivity the citizens of a nation will have.

Family is the core of any society. What happens in the home affects nations! The importance of a strong family unit is monumental, and it is exactly why the devil is always out to steal, kill, and destroy the family unit.

Media (the news, Internet, journalism) provides the link between many of these mountains and the ordinary citizen. This is why media is continuously corrupted by lies, falsehoods, and misdirection, because it is such a vital means of communication.

And Arts, Entertainment, and Celebration (which largely refers to sports). . . .What in the world does *this* do?

Surely watching Judy Garland sing "Over the Rainbow" in *The Wizard of Oz* pales in comparison to governments overseeing the course of history, or educators shaping the minds and thoughts of the next generation.

Wrong!

More than any other mountain, the Arts is the greatest *influencer* of all! Art reveals, reflects, reacts, satirizes. It creates a mirror through which the rest of society can peer inside and see a humorous, sobering, frightening, or even savage reflection of itself.

Art creates trends within culture. In fact, art and culture are virtually synonymous with one another. Fashion, styles, moods, and attitudes are often the direct reflection of a movie star, a celebrity recording artist, a popular television show, or a film genre.

When there is a school shooting or a crime perpetrated by a young person, what is the *first* thing everyone always says?

"It's them there young kids with their violent video games and their Freddy the 13th blood and guts movies they're always watching."

(That's a satirical Appalachian accent, and yes, I know it's actually *Friday the 13th*; Freddy is from *Nightmare on Elm Street*.)

But in all seriousness, it's true. The negative influence of violent video games and gory slasher films are *always* blamed for the violent actions of adolescents; while these are rarely the *only* reasons a young person commits violent acts, there is no denying the powerful influence of these creative mediums.

Why, then, do people often dismiss the Arts as being pleasure-seeking entertainment *only*, and swiftly deny its influential merits?

If we acknowledge it has enough influential power to forcibly cause a teenager to grab a gun and commit unspeakable crimes, then we *have* to acknowledge its potential for positive influence. And not just positive influence. Christ-centered influence.

After all, Jesus Christ has a lot more influential power than Freddy Krueger.

The Arts can influence a person. That person can then influence a family. The family can then influence society, from education all the way to the highest position in government.

It all works together like links in a chain.

Art reaches the emotions and the subconscious. It taps into our longings, our fears, and our innermost desires. It serves as a connecter between the outside world and our "right brain"- typically the side of the brain that houses your feelings, intuitions, and creativity.

Art does NOT work logically, literally, or analytically (and you'll read more about that in the coming chapters). The Hollywood boardroom and commercial art in general suffer immensely from this problem (and, may I say, the mainstream Christian market is in danger of suffering from it, too).

When art becomes analytical, it ceases to be art. And when art is reduced to being only a "commercial product", it loses a lot of its power to affect the right brain and becomes bogged down by "left brain sensibilities"- that is, logic, reason, analysis.

Art does speak, comment, illustrate, and teach, but it does so in an intuitive way and not always in a way that can be properly discussed in an executive board meeting.

Now some artistic purists state that art should *only* be art and should *not* say anything or teach anything. Such purists typically frown upon something like You Connection, which uses art and creativity to communicate the Gospel to audiences. However. . . .

There is no such thing as noncommunicative art!

By its very nature, art speaks, whether the artist wants it to or not. A blob of blue clay says *something*. Even if it makes the observer think, "That's a really stupid piece of art," it inevitably made said observer conscious of good art and bad art, or at the very least it stimulated a reaction. Hence, the blob of blue clay spoke!

The famous author Roald Dahl (author of such children's classics as *Charlie and the Chocolate Factory, James and the Giant Peach, Matilda, Fantastic Mr. Fox,* etc.) once stated that he always intended for his stories to entertain children only and not to teach them anything.

Yet *Charlie and the Chocolate Factory* is one of the most scathing and unapologetic morality tales of 20th Century literature, so true in its darkly hilarious depiction of right and wrong that it remains a controversial book despite its continual worldwide popularity in literature and pop culture.

Even if the author only *intends* to entertain readers, viewers, listeners, or observers, creativity just won't remain confined to such parameters.

Because creativity comes from the right brain, the creator will consciously or subconsciously transfer his or her thoughts, feelings, beliefs, ideals, and innermost desires into the creation.

That's what God did. Genesis states that humans are made in His likeness. An author writes of which he knows.

REACHING OUT THROUGH THE ARTS

It is my belief that art does not reach the masses.

Well, says a naysayer, it certainly does in America.

To which I reply, yes, that's the problem with American art. In fact, that's why a lot of so-called "American art" should be categorized as amusement park attractions.

The giant Hollywood summer blockbuster with its huge CGI effects and its overblown budget and its big celebrity stars is not necessarily a work of art. It is merely an amusement attraction similar to what you experience when you go to Disneyland. It delights and thrills you for the moment, like a roller coaster, and it may say one or two obligatory things about environment, or female empowerment. But it is really nothing more than a commercial amusement intended to create noises and colorful imagery.

True art reaches a person's emotions, soul, and spirit, and that's not always going to appeal to a mass audience. It's going to appeal to. . .well, whoever chooses to connect to it.

Turning art into a mass-produced commercial product basically removes its potency and transforms it into a spectator sport. Football and baseball are much more suitable to be mass audience platforms. You're *supposed* to simply be a spectator and watch who wins and loses the game. It's clear-cut, logical, and satisfying to the left brain.

But art is best when it reaches *pockets* of people at a time. Maybe *this* film reaches *this* group of people, while *that* theatre performance reaches another, and that painting reaches another, and that piece of music another.

My feeling is that you shouldn't even *try* reaching the left-brained, logical, football lover through art and creativity.

Let art reach out to whom it wants.

Didactic art is the use of art to communicate moral instruction as an ulterior motive within the storyline; or simply, it's using art to teach, instruct, or explain.

It dates back to the Greek and Roman passion plays, which were designed to educate the general public on Greek or Roman gods and their (mythological) qualities and characteristics. But it was presented in a highly elaborate way with costumes and masks and special stage effects that were probably quite advanced even for modern times.

Didactic art is certainly the *modus operandi* for You Connection, and probably all the Christian Arts, which usually seeks to inform the audience member about some aspect of God, His principles, or His Word.

To this day, the concept carries a derogatory note, and is often used as a statement of criticism about a play or a film;

"it was too didactic and that spoiled the entertainment of it."

But again, *all* art is didactic to *some* degree. When done properly, didacticism is an extraordinary experience, and in my opinion, the perfect way to *use* creativity.

All things have a purpose, and creativity should not be any exception. The more we *use* creativity, the more people will regard it as a vital part of everyday life.

Art needs to relate, and this is where the Christian church sometimes falls a little short. One of my private rules regarding You Connection (which I can't say I will never break) is to never feature Bible robes or depict Bible times.

This is not to discount groundbreaking projects like Dallas Jenkins' *The Chosen* or other wonderful Bible-era depictions like Mel Gibson's *The Passion of the Christ*.

Those are exceptions because they are unique, innovative, and provide a fresh perspective on the life of Jesus or other biblical figures.

My personal reason for excluding that setting from You Connection is that audiences generally don't find biblical times interesting. It's as simple as that. Very few films or stage plays are based on, say, Roman times or Babylonian times (the most notable are probably the biblical epics of long ago like *Ben-Hur*).

Sorry to say, but aesthetically and creatively, it just doesn't appeal to the imagination like the Middle Ages, with castles and knights in shining armor and fair princesses and dragons and quests to find ancient swords. Or intergalactic battles in faraway galaxies. Or stories set deep in the forest with fairies and elves and evil gnomes. Or time periods like the 1950s, the 1880s, the 1930s.

Imagination is a vital ingredient in any artistic work, and it is important that *Christian* art be relatable. That's why I steer away from depicting traditional Bible stories or ordinary stories about contemporary people in contemporary life. Great though it is, unless you have a fresh take on it, it's just not going to reach people like fantasy or whimsy or other more popular genres and styles.

RECLAIMING THE ARTS

Taking the Arts back for Christ.

The statement is so cliché that it's sadly become a little corny. Though the *intent* of the phrase is excellent, the question remains.

How?

First of all, it takes more than just occasionally releasing a Christian film into cinemas. Call me cynical, but I sometimes find it amusing the way some of my fellow Christian brothers and sisters get *so* excited that a Christian film is going to be playing at the Cinemark down the road for *three whole days* before going to streaming! And the tickets are going *fast*, and you'd better get yours, because this is *so* cool that we're *taking Hollywood back for Christ* and Christians have finally *won the war* against the evils of Hollywood!

Obviously, I am teasing my brethren in good-hearted fashion only. However, the sentiment is often fairly accurate to that. While it's wonderful to have a Christian film get a cinema release, limited or otherwise, we'd be a little naïve to think that this is singlehandedly destroying the evils of Hollywood and proclaiming the superiority of Christianity in cinema forevermore.

In short, it's going to take a little more than *that* to "take the Arts back for Christ."

First, is there any truth to that phrase, "taking the Arts back for Christ"? That seems to suggest that it was stolen from Christ at some point and we need to take it back.

Have the Arts been stolen?

Well. . . .yes and no.

As stated at the beginning of the book, the Arts has always been associated with the secular world, from the Greeks and Romans to gypsies to bawdy music halls to greedy Hollywood executives. So in *that* sense, yes, throughout history, secular society has largely laid claim to the Arts, using it for secular purposes. The church, meanwhile, has largely *criticized* the Arts for being pagan, ungodly, or pleasure-seeking.

So, from that perspective, yes, the Arts needs to be reclaimed for Christ. *The earth is the Lord's and all its fullness (1 Corinthians 10:26).* The pagan world has no rightful claim to anything. We are commissioned by Jesus Himself to make disciples of all nations, and that means laying claim to *all* mountains and spheres of influence.

However, it must also be noted that. . .well, the earth is the Lord's and all its fullness. God is ultimately in sovereign command of everyone and everything. He does not need saving, nor does He need us to claim anything on His behalf. It all belongs to Him already!

Rather, He *chooses* to partner with us to see His kingdom advance on the earth. So, in *that* sense, the battle is already won, and the Arts already belongs to Christ.

We just need to let the rest of the world understand that.

How do you "reclaim" a land, then?

Well, what did the Israelites do when they reached the Promised Land?

They infiltrated!

Claiming or reclaiming territory requires infiltration in ALL areas. Like sending missionaries to a third-world country, Christians must be sent to every corner of the artistic globe. Sure, yes, we need to infiltrate Hollywood, but I do get tired of Christians *always* talking about Hollywood like it's the *only* influential area of the Arts anywhere in the universe.

Broadway needs infiltration, probably even more than Hollywood, as it has long been a hive for the ungodly, immoral, and unprincipled.

Community theatre needs it, and so do other forms of media and streaming. Though contemporary Christian music still thrives, there is a call for more.

We need people inside the industry *and* outside of it. That is, we need godly people in the highest levels of Hollywood, Broadway, and media, but also in the independent world- such as independent film, local theatre, or the indie music scene.

In fact, I believe we need to focus more attention on the independent side of the Arts (and yes, I am saying that because that's what You Connection does, so this is perhaps a biased opinion).

While a Christian producer within the halls of the Hollywood elite can do a tremendous amount of good, there are thousands of other ways regional groups, independent companies, and local artists can reach their communities, states, or localized public with the Gospel, in ways that the Christian Hollywood producer can't.

Reclaiming means *total* infiltration, and that only happens when Christians invade the Arts on a local, statewide, nationwide, and worldwide basis.

That's why I like to look beyond just the one Christian film that happens to get a limited release in the cinema. That's wonderful, and we need that, too. But the local Christian indie filmmaker who releases his or her film onto YouTube has just as much of an opportunity to reclaim the Arts for Christ!

Bottom line, we need it all. Big and small, high places and low places, from the small civic theatre to the Academy Awards.

In order to properly infiltrate territory, you also have to *know the land you're trying to claim.*

The Israelites did that, too, sending in spies to Jericho to scout out the land. Incidentally, they did so by using the services of a prostitute, who incidentally and ironically is now Jesus' great-great-great-great-great-great grandmother (as far as His *earthly* genealogy goes, that is).

This is no accident, because God loves redemption.

It also illustrates an important aspect of "reclaiming the Arts", one in which many within the body of Christ fall a little short.

You've got to study the land you wish to occupy, and I do think that sometimes the church is a little clumsy in its well-intentioned efforts to utilize the Arts for God's purposes.

Often times a film or even a live presentation is produced by a big ministry or a megachurch, simply because they can afford it and would like to try to reach out in that way. Unfortunately, a pastor or ministry leader may know little (or nothing) about the Arts- its history, its styles, its trends- resulting in a product that *looks* artistic, but lacks any true artistic merits (such as good acting, good writing, etc.).

These kinds of well-meaning products abound on Christian streaming sites, and while they might be praised by non-artistic churchgoers, they are heavily criticized or mocked by the secular world, and even a lot of Christians (myself included) don't respond to them because. . .they're just not very well-made.

So, what does it mean to know the land you're trying to claim? It means:

~ Knowing its history ~

Do Christian producers know about Menippean or Juvenalian Satire? Do they know what *"deux ex machina"* is in a story? What about *katascopia* (also known as experimental fantasticality)? What is a *panto*, an unreliable narrator, or a kitchen sink drama? Steampunk? Deiselpunk?

Answer: This is the history of the Arts. These are just a few of the many styles, genres, concepts, and storytelling elements that have been employed for centuries by countless playwrights, authors, and dramatists, from Shakespeare to Steven Spielberg.

It is vital that the Arts be reclaimed by Christians who have a firm understanding of its great history and grand traditions!

This is emphasized because, as stated, a mega-ministry may have the money to fund a Christian project (such as a film that gets a limited release in a cinema), but if the producers have no knowledge of the grand traditions, they will fail in their attempt to produce a work of art that is of comparable artistic quality to secular art.

Even if the camera is doing something technically correct, and the lighting is technically the appropriate level of brightness, the film (if we are using a film as an example) will merely come off as a *copycat* of a secular film.

People who respond to the Arts can *tell* if something has artistic merit, or whether the producer or artist has any real knowledge of the medium in which they are working.

And budget does not disguise it, either. I've seen plenty of big budget productions, Christian and secular, that had virtually no understanding of any look, feeling, genre, or style.

~ Knowing its language ~

In the same manner, you have to "know the language" of the land you're attempting to claim. You have to know how to talk to the people in the land, how to interact with them.

The Israelite spies had to know how to temporarily immerse themselves into Jericho culture without compromising themselves or their faith. They couldn't talk to Rahab like they talked to their fellow Israelites. She was a prostitute. More than likely they had to be a little more "streetwise" in their speech.

This is why it is so important for Christians to embrace all styles within the Arts, which has never been an easy thing for the church to do. Opposition to Christian rock music in the 1970s was huge, and genres like fantasy continue to be controversial within Christian circles (though this has subsided a little since the 1980s).

The devil doesn't own an electric guitar, or any creative or literary genre. Fantasy, when handled well, can create an extraordinary symbolic representation of the supernatural world, and the battle between angels and demons, light and dark.

A knife can be used to murder someone. But it is also used to eat, and a surgeon uses it to save lives. The knife itself is a dumb object. It's how you *use* the knife that makes the difference. The same is true with artistic things.

This is why You Connection abstains from Bible robes. We want to speak the language of the people we're trying to reach, and that means going *hardcore artsy*, and at the same time, going *hardcore Gospel*.

Frank Peretti's *This Present Darkness* and *Piercing the Darkness* are masterpieces in fusing the Gospel with the classic traditions of the Arts.

The genre is basically supernatural horror. It has all the elements of classic horror film and horror literature- demonic and supernatural entities, jump scares, heart-pounding intensity, chilling mysteries, and quite a few genuinely terrifying moments (particularly with little demon-possessed Amber Brandon in *Piercing the Darkness*, a striking similarity to the equally demon-possessed Regan MacNeil in *The Exorcist*).

The great difference is that Peretti's horror features the *winning* side, as well. Secular horror has no such fortune. Instead of the demonic forces overpowering everyone like in any classic horror story, in Peretti's world the *demons* are in turn overpowered by angels and the far more superior power of Christ.

This is knowing both the history and the language of the Arts at its absolute finest, and I personally consider the *Darkness* books to be among the greatest works in the entire history of Christian Arts, right beside *Pilgrim's Progress* or *Mere Christianity*.

It is also an example of the third thing to know when claiming or reclaiming land.

~ Knowing the battle ~

American Christianity has been particularly notorious in its debate over spiritual warfare and God's supernatural intervention in our daily lives.

As this book is not an apologetic on that subject, I will sum it all up in one sentence.

It's time for the American church to read the Word of God and believe it!

In order to reclaim the Arts, you have to know that we are in a supernatural battle. Jesus has already won the victory through the cross, but we are still in a daily war with the devil and his legions, until whatever consummation occurs.

Furthermore, the Holy Spirit was sent to us after Jesus ascended to heaven, for the purpose of empowering us to be ministers to all the nations of the earth. Nothing has passed away, and the gifts of the Spirit are as active today as they were at Pentecost. We *need* the Holy Spirit in our daily lives to *speak to us and move through us*.

And we are called to take the Gospel to every corner of the globe, and not simply to be passive, moral citizens of society.

If you do not believe any of that, then you won't have much success "taking the Arts back for Christ" or taking *anything* back for Christ. If you believe there are no spiritual gifts, there is no empowerment of the Spirit, and there is no heavenly war, then what's the point of claiming land? Just be a nice, moral citizen.

But if you believe that God has called us to be His ambassadors on the earth, then you know *every* land is worth fighting for. And He has "thoroughly equipped us for every good work" (2 Timothy 3:17).

BE THE MUSIC MAKERS

One of my favorite films is 1971's *Willy Wonka and the Chocolate Factory*, based on the Roald Dahl novel of the (almost) same name; I am a fan of all classic literature for both adults and children, such as *Oliver Twist, Alice's Adventures in Wonderland, A Little Princess, The Old Curiosity Shop, Martin Chuzzlewit (Dickens' least remembered novel which I think is great), all the works of George MacDonald, etc.* Again, if Christians are going to take ground, we've got to be well versed in all aspects of artistic culture.

As to the 1971 *Willy Wonka* adaptation, I still find this film extremely unique and original, with its stream-of-consciousness style and delightfully clunky, unstructured pacing to its funny but searing morality tale, and how well it blends didacticism and whimsy. I also love how it stood out as perhaps the most unique "family film" of its time, coming out during the turbulent early 1970s when family films weren't being made except for Disney (and *Willy Wonka* is far too funky, hip, and edgy to have been compared to a Disney film of the era).

One of Willy Wonka's quips (which actually comes from the poem *Ode* by Arthur O'Shaughnessy) is, "We are the music makers, and we are the dreamers of dreams."

That was a long explanation just to give a backstory for that one phrase, which could almost be a Bible verse.

Of course, this is *not* a Bible verse, but it's about as close to one as you can get. The Bible *does* say that as followers of Christ we are "a chosen generation, a royal priesthood, a holy nation, His own special people" (1 Peter 2:9), and that we are to "do the work of an evangelist, and fulfill our ministry" (2 Timothy 4:5).

So that's *basically* "we are the music makers, and we are the dreamers of dreams."

It is the followers of Christ who are called to be the innovators! We should be the trendsetters, the gamechangers, the setters of the rules. The secular world should be turning to *us* and copying *our* styles and fashions and trends.

Certainly, there will always be people who will oppose God because "in this world you will have tribulation" (John 16:33). But the body of Christ has a bad habit of pulling *away* from the world, of isolating itself from culture and society. This makes the followers of Christ ignorant of the current language of the world, and it also makes the world assume that Christianity has no place in society.

Christianity is the *foundation* of society, because Jesus is the foundation of *all things!* He is the "chief cornerstone, and there is no salvation in any other, for there is no other name under heaven given among men by which we must be saved" (Acts 4:11-12).

Let's be the inventors! The forerunners! The creators! The founders! Let's be the ones making the music, and the ones who are dreaming the dreams.

Practically speaking, one of the ways to be a "music maker" and a "dreamer of dreams" in the world of the Arts is to simply *bust loose!*

That is, let's get creative!

We already know that God is a creative God. As stated, Christian art (particularly Christian film) has a tendency to be predictable, contemporary, and, shall we say, a little bland in the creative department.

I see massively creative content on Netflix and other secular streaming sites that far outshines some of the gentler, Sunday School-style content found on Christian streaming. That's not to downplay the content or its message. It is simply that secular art still pushes the creative boundaries far better than the majority of the Christian market.

One reason is that Christian art is deemed more marketable by many producers if it *looks* Christian. If it looks like something from the Marvel Cinematic Universe, then people might not know it's Christian and that's just *way* too confusing (and potentially offensive, according to some producers).

Another reason why Christians don't always bust loose creatively is, I think, *religiosity*. Perhaps a lot of Christian artists are *eager* to create a kind of Christian version of Tim Burton's *The Nightmare Before Christmas*, or the Gospel equivalent to Quentin Tarantino's *From Dusk Till Dawn*. But then they get felled by that old religious voice that whispers "you can't glorify God through *that* kind of art".

Well, if we *don't* glorify God, then the rocks will cry out (Luke 19), and I'm certainly not going to be one-upped by a rock.

Again, it's the knife analogy. The knife is a dumb object. It's how you *use* the knife that makes all the difference.

SO NOW WHAT?

The big question after reading all this:
So what do we do now?
The Arts is a field that is truly white unto harvest, but as Jesus Himself said, "the harvest is truly great, but the laborers are few" (Luke 10:2).

Of all the seven mountains, the Arts is by far the least attended to by the body of Christ. We give to missionaries and soup kitchens, and scores of other kinds of ministries, but rarely ever think of giving to the Arts.

That's the first "now what". ***Christian Arts needs more financial support from the body of Christ.***
This will only happen when more and more Christians begin *to see the Arts as a viable means of evangelism,* worthy to be included alongside foreign missions or social work. The more we can break the stigma of art as being "pleasure-seeking entertainment" only, the more people will sow into Christian artistic endeavors.

And the only way for *that* to happen is more and more Christian artists need to *demonstrate* the viability of art and Gospel, Jesus and creativity, theology and theatrics.

Another aspect to gaining more respect for the Arts is making non-artistic people aware of the *professional* world of the Arts. The average non-artistic pragmatist tends to think that Hollywood and Broadway are the only two places on the planet where anyone does anything artistic. Beyond that, the Arts is nothing but local dance studios and acting programs for young people. (I have nothing against those things, but those are entirely different industries. At best, they are training programs to help young people learn how they can *integrate* into the professional world of the Arts; at the very least, they are fun after-school programs.)

There is a vast professional world of the Arts far beyond New York and LA, from indie filmmaking to media companies to professional live theatre to indie music to a myriad of other kinds of art galleries, performance groups, Internet content producers. All of this is viable, professional work being done in the marketplace. Contrary to popular thought, the Arts is actually a thriving industry to get into, and the more we raise the awareness, the more the average non-artistic Christian will want to support it.

In that same vein, ***we need more creative Christians who are willing to surrender their talents to Christ***. I went through this as a teenager during a powerful move of God in the early-to-mid 1990s. I remember moments of being on my face in the presence of God, telling Him that I would give all these creative talents over to Him, to either use or discard, as long as He would use me for His plans and purposes.

Be *ready* to surrender, because boy, oh, boy, does God take you up on it!

Creative people can be very possessive of their talents, because, after all, creation is a very personal exchange. Any artistic person knows it's not just a functional activity. Your creativity is part of *who you are*. It's a part of your whole DNA. Most importantly, it's a part of how God created you.

So it's a big deal for a creative person to hand over such things to God. What if He takes it all away from you? What if He uses your talents in a way you don't like?

All these thoughts can easily swarm in the artistic person's mind, sometimes resulting in a highly creative Christian who is choosing to go their own path rather than God's path.

But God didn't give creative people talents only to take them all away. He *will* use that creativity, and we desperately need more believers making the decision to partner with God in their skills and talents.

I can say from personal experience, you won't regret it. I am regularly exhausted from the endless stream of creativity the Holy Spirit stirs inside me on a daily basis. I don't have the nerve to tell Him to slow down.

We need more artistic people at the helm of artistic projects. This is actually true for the secular world of the Arts as well as the Christian world.

I don't care for people who say, "artistic people have no business sense", and I typically don't associate with would-be collaborators who place such a derogatory stereotype on my shoulders.

There is a different pulse and rhythm to artistic-oriented business that ordinary marketplace businesspeople have trouble understanding. Therefore, they simply say "artistic people are crazy", an easy way to avoid having to learn the necessary business skills required for artistic-oriented endeavors.

This attitude often results in the Arts being run like a corporate entity rather than a creative one (a big problem today in "corporate Hollywood"). A lot of businesspeople believe creativity ought to be shoved into existing business models that computer companies and cereal manufacturers and retailers use. Hey, it works for *them!* Look at these flow charts and statistics!

But what works for Apple and Kellogg's Corn Flakes may not necessarily work for film, theatre, music, etc.

There *is* a great deal of business in the Arts, because the Arts *is* a business, even if you're using it to minister the Gospel. Sure, there might be wild painters or kooky musicians or scatterbrained writers out there who haven't got the first clue how to butter their own bread, let alone think logically about business ideas.

Then again, there are plenty of wild executives and kooky board members and scatterbrained corporate managers who *also* haven't got a clue how to butter their own bread, let alone think logically about business ideas.

So the "artistic people have no business sense" attitude is a stereotype that has been popularized by non-artistic businesspeople who don't understand the Arts.

It is advisable to stay away from such people when dealing with artistic-oriented endeavors, in the same way that you should avoid a plumber who doesn't know anything about plumbing.

While the Arts *is* a business and an industry like any other, at the same time, it is a business and an industry like *no* other.

Organization, management, and pragmatism are all necessary for successful artistic achievements, and to say that *NO* artistic people possess such skills is a lie. (This is like saying, "All blonde girls are bimbos." Perhaps there is this one girl you know who really *is* a "bimbo", but you are using that one girl as the ultimate standard for *all* women with blonde hair, mainly fueled by the notorious "blonde bimbo" stereotype that has been popularized in society over the years.)

People seem to forget that *you have to be organized simply to create a piece of art!*

Writing a song, creating a painting, choreographing a dance, directing a play, filming a movie. . .You can't exactly do any of these things on a whim and a fancy and a crazy artistic impulse.

The point is, I believe the Arts is a unique *form* of business that should have its *own* standards, rules, and measures that are *separate* and *distinct* from traditional business practices.

Elements like risk, innovation, creative expression, and artistic merit are VITAL to any artistic-oriented endeavor. But these are elements that are *shunned* by the traditional businessperson, who values certainty, predictability, and profitability above any notions of "trying something new" or "going in a different direction".

But innovation is the backbone of the Arts. Always has been and always will be. Art is used to create. That means making something that didn't exist before.

Bottom line: Yes, there is plenty of pragmatic thinking involved in the Arts, but the ones doing the pragmatic thinking need to *understand the Arts*- how it works, how it moves, how it succeeds.

It works best when you have someone who is both artistic and pragmatic, and contrary to popular belief, there are *plenty* of those who exist.

Or if ordinary businesspeople are involved in an artistic project, they need to have a love or a passion for the Arts, either possessing some artistic skills themselves or being ardent patrons of the Arts.

Trying to get the Arts to squeeze into standard business models is literally the proverbial "trying to fit a square peg into a round hole."

Personally, I am more of a visionary and an innovator who has artistic skills, so I actually consider myself to be a businessman. By the grace of God, I built You Connection from the ground up and for the whole of a decade, did just about every single task myself, from paying the bills and organizing the shooting schedules to writing, directing, acting, and administering both the production and ministry aspects of the organization.

A "crazy artistic person" cannot do that.

Finally, *we need to redefine quality*. This is also true in the secular world as well as Christian. It's just a true statement about the Arts, particularly in the Western part of the world.

In particular, the Arts in America has become nothing more than Disneyland-style spectacle. Hollywood films are mostly an overload of headache-inducing special effects, impossibly wild editing, and ridiculously implausible storylines. Even Broadway has largely leaned into the "bigger and better" attitude with enormous sets and tremendous thrills and spectacles.

All this does is cheapen the Arts and reinforce the notion of the Arts as being nothing but big, loud, dumb entertainment. Big isn't bad. But if that's *all* that's promoted, that's all people will think of it.

In the case of film, we have fortunately seen the tremendous rise of online streaming, which allows for small, low budget movies to find a fresh new outlet. People don't expect extravagance online; they just expect a good story.

But getting more specific, there is sometimes a danger in the Christian world of having the *tools* but not the *talent*. Using film as another example, I have seen a number of Christian films that seem to have a pretty experienced DP (Director of Photography), and the editing looks pretty tight, and the scenes look like a regular Hollywood scene and are kind of staged that way, too.

Unfortunately, the actors sound like they're reading off of cue cards, the dialogue is so corny you could sell the harvest of corn and retire while young, and the plot that unfolds is so predictable that the good camerawork and the solid editing don't really mean anything. It *looks* good, but the content *sucks*.

Hence, we need to *redefine quality*. Yes, the technical aspects of a work of art need to be professional and excellent (*especially* when it comes to Christian art), but I think a lot of the Arts community (both secular and Christian) gets easily lulled into the notion that if it looks technically good, that means it's quality work.

Not so.

Just watch an expert actor reciting a well-written monologue with no lights or sets or props, and you will quickly realize that **quality is in the content.**

The technical aspects of a work of art merely *reinforce* the quality of the content. But true quality is found in the skill of the performer, the depth of the writing, the uniqueness of the storytelling, the perspective of the painting, the structure of the song, the personality of the singer.

And all these qualities have nothing to do with the size of a budget. These are the qualities of a creative person.

Why is it important to redefine quality? So that we can embrace *all* of the Arts regardless of its size, shape, budget, or level of spectacle. If a work of art can only be a gigantic show with pyrotechnics and huge effects, then two-thirds of the artistic community will be left out in the cold.

The Arts has always been a financially impoverished mountain, and reducing "quality" to big budget amusements not only prevents true artisans from displaying their talents, but also robs the world of true art.

Low budget doesn't mean low quality. There *can* be things that are low budget *and* low quality, but then, there are *plenty* of things that are high budget but low quality, too.

True art isn't lights and smoke. It's the grandmother sitting by the fireplace in a time gone by, quietly knitting and saying to her little grandchildren, "Let me tell you a story. It happened long ago, in a kingdom very far away. . . ."

YOU CONNECTION: ANSWERING THE CALL

Though this can easily be misconstrued as a cheap plug for the author's own company, it is *also* meant to reveal some ways that You Connection is *doing* the various things mentioned in this discourse. We are active participants in this dynamic fusion of Gospel and creativity, and my heart is to see a greater appreciation of the Arts within the body of Christ, as a viable and effective means of communicating the reality of Christ to a world that needs Him now more than ever before.

You Connection is essentially the "brand name" for a variety of endeavors including films and the YC Web streaming site, live theatre presentation in the Dallas, Texas, area, and other efforts to raise the awareness and understanding of Christian Arts.

It is a 501(c)(3) nonprofit company; hence, we are mainly donation-based, rather than investor-based or revenue-based. Crowdfunding is, in my opinion, one of the best alternative ways of funding the Arts in our present day. It allows the independent artist the opportunity of producing his or her work without having to wait for big investments to come in.

In our case, it also demonstrates the fusion of *art* and *ministry*; or rather, using art *as* ministry. This way You Connection is not classified, or dismissed, as commercial art.

Of course, I have nothing against commercial art. You Connection is simply here to show that there *can* be other ways of doing it. Let's not just get locked into the same way of marketing, or the same way of distributing. It's really just a way to demonstrate how art can be used for ministry purposes; perhaps it's even our way of *proving* it.

Let's be innovators. Let's be dreamers of dreams.

In fact, You Connection is *all about invention!* I am all about being unique, being different, standing out from the crowd, creating something fresh. That's not just a Gospel-oriented thing. That's something we need in the Arts! That's what makes a work of art exciting. It does something new and different. It isn't just cereal boxes, all exactly the same, lined up neatly in a row at the supermarket.

You Connection films are intentionally experimental-style and uniquely structured, with slightly older fashioned camerawork similar to 1960s, 1970s, and 1980s cinema, and jangly, non sequitur editing. Like pure indie films, the focus is always on character, performance, story, message, and feeling.

You Connection theatre presentations are a curious hybrid of immersive, interactive, experimental, and musical theatre, with characters interacting with the audience in an intimate setting where the seats are interspersed with the sets, placing the audience in the middle of the action. We adhere mostly to the Brechtian technique. (Ironically, Bertolt Brecht was a Marxist theatre practitioner in East Berlin during the Cold War era, but he *did* create a great non-traditional theatre technique; let's not forget the Israelite spies used a prostitute to help them stay undercover in Jericho.)

You Connection regularly fuses classic genres and styles with deep Gospel teaching to create a work of art that is equally theological and equally artistic.

Like George MacDonald, who used literature to not only express strong theological principles but to also educate his readers on history, literature, and folklore, a You Connection presentation seeks to celebrate (or even introduce) the great traditions of the Arts while pulling those traditions into the Kingdom of God and His righteousness (and using them for His purposes rather than secular purposes, just as Frank Peretti did with supernatural horror, or George MacDonald and C.S. Lewis with fairy tales and fantasy).

Examples include the YC Web film *Escape from the Grand Guignol*, referring to the real Grand Guignol theatre, a horror theatre in France from the late 1800s to the mid-20th Century. The film not only uses the history of the real theatre as a basis for its plot, but also inserts subliminal references such as "hot and cold showers" which *only* a viewer with knowledge of Grand Guignol shows would understand. Additionally, the "insane asylum" was a common location in Grand Guignol plays and is the central locale for the film, in an inverted scenario of Christians being confined to an institution so that the "experts" may cure them of their "insanity".

Rainbow Shoes is a pure experimental film (in the oddest sense of the word) that follows the classic British pantomime, featuring such classic "panto" elements as the pantomime dame, the boy and girl heroes, the dastardly villain (in this case, literally the devil), and the harlequin narrators. American viewers might not get it, but YC Web is global, with regular viewership from Britain; therefore, a British viewer might easily see the pantomime parallels (a staple of British culture since the 1800s).

Further films like *Little Crooked House* and *Bubblegum Dream Machine* depict the 1950s and 1960s respectively, but not as biographical films. Instead, both present an intentionally phony "pop culture" world that everyone remembers from television and nostalgia, with *Little Crooked House* emulating late 50s television like *Father Knows Best, The Twilight Zone*, and *The Colgate Comedy Hour*, and *Bubblegum Dream Machine* playing out like an episode of *The Monkees* or *The Archies*, with elements of *A Hard Day's Night* and *H.R. Pufnstuf* sprinkled in.

Both film and theatre productions often fuse multiple genres together at a time to create a unique hybrid, merging musicals with drama and surrealism with theological apologetics.

This isn't just done for the sake of being creatively innovative. People pay more attention when they *don't* know what's coming. By creating something unique, you give your audience a chance to really explore the themes, concepts, and ideas presented in your project. They *have* to, because they've never seen a project quite like this, and they cannot predict what the next scene is going to be.

As a nonprofit, You Connection rarely has adequate money for *anything*. So we use this to our advantage by being as creative as we possibly can, because. . .that's what the Arts is all about. Being creative. Our emphasis is always on the *quality* items- the writing, the acting, the telling of the tale. There is a liberating energy to having a small budget, and even with more funds on future projects, a lot of our methods will likely stay the same.

Hence, *You Connection strongly champions the world small budget Arts!*

This was something I struggled with for years after I graduated from high school, since filmmaking was a huge part of my interest. It was the late 1990s, so streaming wasn't yet a thing, DVDs had only just come out, and it took several years (into the mid-2000s) for digital technology to become available to the average, low-incomed individual.

The struggle was that I didn't have twenty million dollars in my back pocket, and that seemed to be the *only* way to make or distribute a film.

It actually wasn't until the launch of You Connection, and the advent of streaming media online, that I was able to resurrect the filmmaker side of me. The Internet accommodates a wide variety of media that *can* be produced at a low cost (without sacrificing true quality- writing, acting, etc.), because people are not watching the content on giant Cinemark screens, but on their phones, tablets, laptops, or at the very grandest, their flat screen TV.

In both the secular *and* Christian arenas, **we need to shine a spotlight on independent and low budget productions.** There are so many talented artists out there, and a lot of them are waiting to be given a million dollar check before they *think* they can realize their projects (particularly in performing and visual art).

You Connection is out to prove that you *can* have excellent quality and powerful impact with "shoestrings, duct tape, and popsicle sticks". Just be creative!

Big is great if you've got the money, but as the old dictum goes, "art thrives on restrictions." Emphasizing *content* over *budget* will allow more and more artists from all walks of life to use their skills in amazing ways, without having to wait for the "big producer" to come along. As stated, let's *redefine quality!*

Finally, You Connection exists in the marketplace, not within the four walls of the church. This is not anything extraordinary, and tons of other Christian organizations are the same.

But it's very important that You Connection theatre shows are performed at our facility in the hub of a vibrant urban area in Dallas, Texas, and that YC Web is available online, all over the world.

Again, so is Pure Flix and countless other Christian entities, but a lot of art does tend to get relegated to church or church-related arenas (musicians do worship bands instead of ordinary Christian bands, churches produce their own theatrical presentations within their own church, etc.).

Church life is great, and we all *need* to be in fellowship with our community of believers. But it's the Arts *out here in the big wide world* that needs reclaiming.

It's being done, but not with nearly as much support, fervor, and energy as in the other six mountains of influence. The Arts is usually treated more as "give or take". If someone produces a work of art that ministers to others, fine. But there is often no *concerted* effort to infiltrate the Arts and use the infiltration to further fulfill Jesus' Great Commission to "go into all the world and preach the Gospel to every creature" (Mark 16).

Let everything that has breath praise the Lord (Psalms 150:6). Isn't that how God created? He spoke and there it was.

Creation is like a breath of life.

You Connection is a 501(c)(3) nonprofit company using professional media and theatre to connect audiences of all ages to the Gospel of Jesus Christ, designed to make audiences think- to challenge secular norms, convict the soul, and proclaim the truth of Christ.

YC has a highly unique brand of creativity, based on the singular style of Founder/Director Matt Kramer, that draws from experimental film, experimental theatre, musicals, whimsy, satire, allegory, and classical storytelling, using the great traditions of the arts to effectively minister.

You Connection targets an "ageless demographic", appealing to a broad spectrum of ages, from adults to teens to grade-school-aged kids.

Main site: www.youconnection.org
YC Web streaming site: www.youconnectionweb.org

Founder/Director Matt Kramer worked in professional television, award-winning videography, performing arts, church ministry, and book publishing for two decades before launching You Connection in 2013, after several attempts over previous years, having conceived an idea like You Connection when he graduated from high school. He has been a passionate follower of Christ since age seven, and a lifelong resident of Dallas, Texas.

Made in the USA
Monee, IL
13 October 2025